# THE ROYAL RIVER

- an aerial guide -

George Sainsbury

Text by Olive Sainsbury

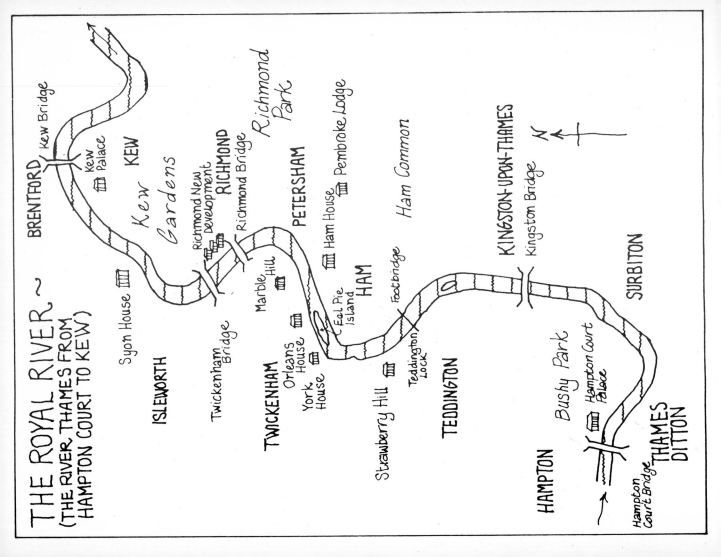

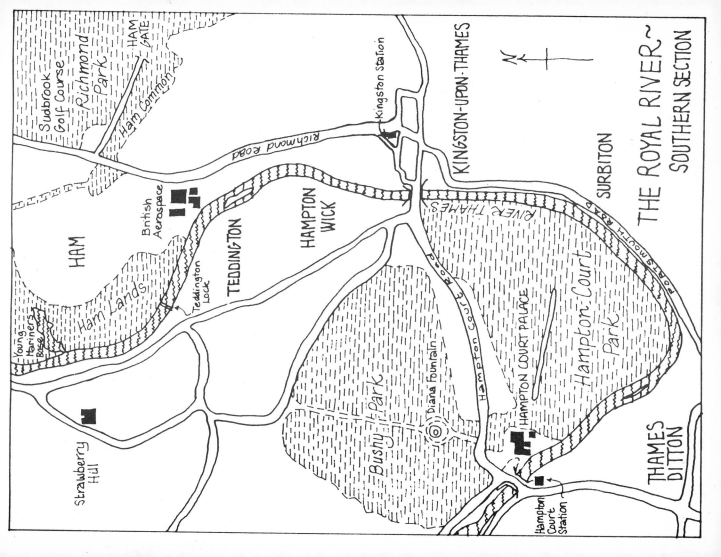

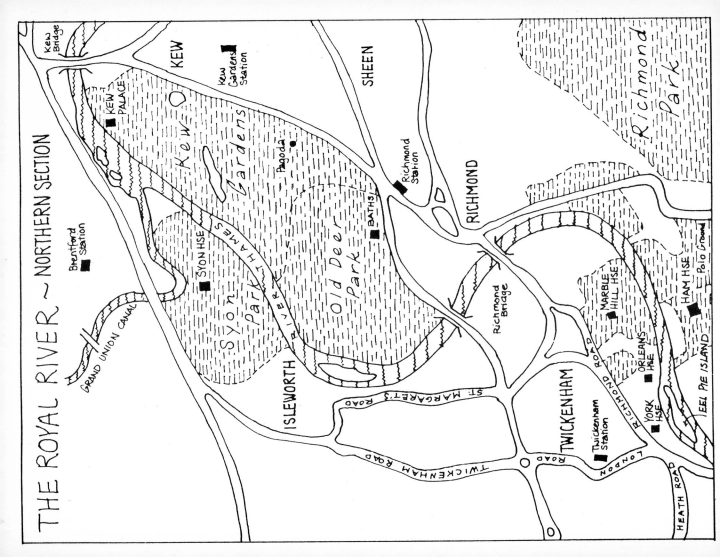

# THE ROYAL RIVER

From Hampton Court to Kew, Richmond's glorious riverside.

When the Queen sailed up the river to open the new Richmond Development on October 28th 1988, accompanied by her scarlet-coated bargemen, she was retracing journeys made by the first Elizabeth, and by several other sovereigns, including Charles II, William & Mary, George II, George III and George IV.

Few parts of London enjoy such beautiful scenes as does Richmond with its quintessential English riverside - fresh and appealing in spring, when the green flush is on the trees, splendid and serene in its summer maturity, misty and mysterious in winter, when the many noble buildings of the past can be seen in their full splendour.

# HAMPTON COURT TO KINGSTON-ON-THAMES

As the River Thames enters the borough of Richmond at Hampton, it begins an enormous bend which swings south and then turns northwards towards Kingston. This meander contains two large open spaces, Hampton Court Park and Bushy Park, and, standing between them on the north bank of the river, the first of the noble palaces which grace Richmond's riverside:-

## Hampton Court Palace

Though it was first conceived and built by Cardinal Wolsey in 1514, it was Henry VIII, his royal patron, who enlarged the house and made it a luxurious residence where all his wives (except the unfortunate Catherine of Aragon) resided in turn. Henry also enlarged the park, greatly enjoying the healthy country air, which was to be a great attraction to the royal family at later times when plague rendered London dangerous and distasteful.

Later sovereigns Edward VI, Mary I, Elizabeth, James I and Charles I all held court there. Charles II after his restoration in 1660 planned extensions to the gardens on a large scale, perhaps with Versailles in mind. But by the time William & Mary came to the throne the palace was nearly 200 years old and ripe for renovation.

William and Mary were keen to settle at Hampton Court, where the pure air promised better conditions than foggy London for the king, who suffered from asthma. They chose Sir Christopher Wren, architect of St Pauls, to plan the rebuilding.

Wren's first plan would have demolished most of the original Tudor building, but in the end a more modest design was adopted. The classical renaissance style used for the east facade gives a quite different appearance from the Tudor palace of Henry VII seen from the west.

The Baroque State Apartments were also designed by Wren. Mary concentrated on the gardens, her great interest, and added orange trees as a symbol of the House of Orange, together with many exotic plants brought from America.

In Queen Anne's time the Great Maze was laid out, while decorations to the interior continued to be made to suit the taste of Anne and the first two Georges. George I frequently travelled by river to London and back, and Handel's "Water Music", currently so familiar from a certain TV commercial, was written in honour of these journeys.

George II spent time at Hampton Court every summer, and in his later years was a frequent visitor to Marble Hill House, built for his mistress Henrietta Howard, Countess of Suffolk.

Thereafter the Palace was never occupied by a reigning sovereign, and Queen Victoria finally opened the palace and its gardens to the public in 1837.

The State Rooms at Hampton Court are on the first floor, and contain much that is of interest. On the floor above are "grace and favour" apartments where much damage was inflicted by the fire of 1986. This has resulted in another extensive period of rebuilding.

VISITS: *THE PALACE IS OPEN MID-MARCH - MID-OCTOBER, 9.30 - 18.00; MID - OCTOBER - MID-MARCH, 9.30 - 16.30. CLOSED 23RD - 26TH DEC AND 1ST JAN.*

**The Gardens** at Hampton Court are extensive, laid out in formal paths, lawns and flowerbeds. The so-called "Tudor Gardens" were re-designed in the 18th century, while the Knot Garden was designed and planted in 1924 to exemplify a late 16th century garden. Near the Lower Orangery (built for Queen Anne) is the great vine brought as a cutting from an Essex garden and planted in 1769. Through a gateway in the high brick wall one may pass into the Wilderness, and near the Lion Gate on the main road can be seen the Maze, planted in Queen Anne's reign and formed of 6-foot tall close-clipped hedges.

The famous chestnut avenue in Bushy Park with the great Diana fountain in the centre, was originally planned as the main land ward approach to the Palace. Wren had the fountain, with its bronze Diana, nymphs and dolphins, moved from the palace gardens, regilded and re-erected in the long avenue, but the grand design connecting this to Hampton Court was never carried out.

## Kingston to Petersham

The river takes on a different aspect as it runs northwards under Kingston bridge, where timber yards and boatyards change the character of the riverbanks. Regattas and boat races are held at different times in the summer both at Kingston and Twickenham.

Kingston occupies a site which has been continuously occupied since Saxon times, and indeed the excavation of the river frontage which preceded the present-day building and remoulding of the town centre, revealed the sites of mediaeval shops. The old Coronation stone on which seven Saxon kings were reputedly crowned, now stands near the Guildhall.

Part of the old centre of Kingston is seen in the view of page 10 which shows in the bottom left-hand corner, the old Apple Market, and part of the modern market place. Between these is a complex of narrow alleys and buildings, some of which date back several hundred years. As is commonly the case in English towns with a long history, buildings are frequently re-fronted and even rebuilt, the present Laura Ashley shop being a case in point, while the 'Next' building on the other side of the Market Place was refronted in the 1930s with a deliberate attempt to recreate the old banqueting hall.

On either side of Eden Street, more modern development has taken place, seen in the multi-storey car park and the shopping mall which centres on a square (open to the sky) where one can sit, and this is surrounded by typical 1990s high street shops such as Boots, BHS, Marks & Spencer, Habitat, Hennes etc. The new DHSS building, next to the Post Office, is the most recent addition to this central area.

The recent pedestrianisation of Clarence Street has reinforced Kingston's position as a shopping centre, now much improved by the elegant and attractive interior of the new Bentall's building. The huge new John Lewis building will add new dimensions of shopping and, from the customers' point of view, a useful element of competition.

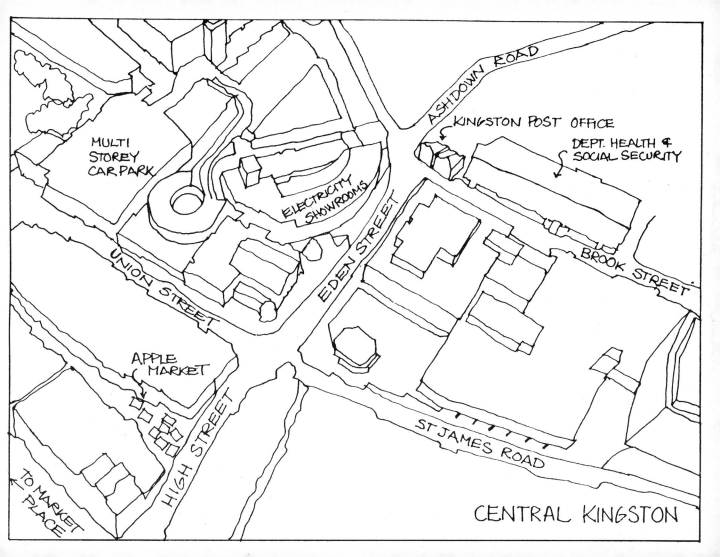

MULTI STOREY CAR PARK

ASHDOWN ROAD

KINGSTON POST OFFICE

DEPT. HEALTH & SOCIAL SECURITY

ELECTRICITY SHOWROOMS

EDEN STREET

UNION STREET

BROOK STREET

APPLE MARKET

HIGH STREET

TO MARKET PLACE

ST JAMES ROAD

CENTRAL KINGSTON

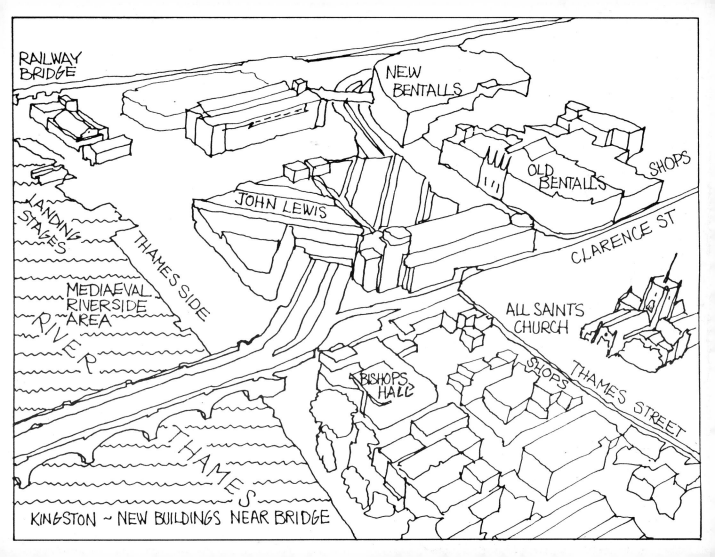

RAILWAY BRIDGE

NEW BENTALLS

OLD BENTALLS

SHOPS

CLARENCE ST

LANDING STAGES

THAMES SIDE

JOHN LEWIS

MEDIAEVAL RIVERSIDE AREA

RIVER

ALL SAINTS CHURCH

THAMES STREET

BISHOPS HALL

SHOPS

THAMES

KINGSTON ~ NEW BUILDINGS NEAR BRIDGE

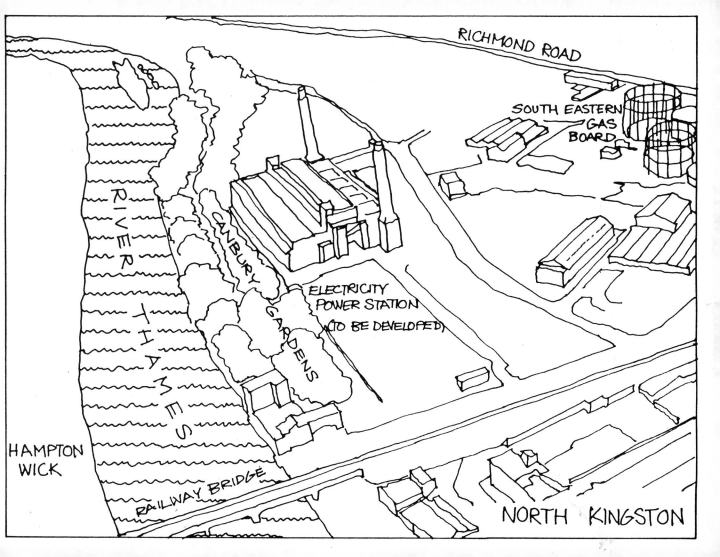

**The Thamesside footpath** which can be followed around Hampton Court Park up to Kingston Bridge, can now be continued on the right bank via Canbury Gardens up to Ham Lands, and then via Petersham Meadows to Richmond. It is possible to follow the river downstream all the way to Hammersmith, with a short break at Barnes.

After Kingston Bridge the next meander of the Thames encompasses **Ham and Petersham,** both of which are bounded by the vast expanses of Richmond Park on the Eastern side. The flat area west of Ham Street was formerly dotted with numerous gravel pits which were exploited by the Dysart family till 1952. The Young Mariners' Base occupies the only remaining lake and Ham Lands stretch alongside the river from **Teddington Lock** to Ham House grounds (see picture on page 19).

At Teddington Lock is a footbridge where pedestrians and cyclists can cross the river at what is the only crossing-place between Richmond and Kingston bridges (barring the ferry at Ham.)

The river here is about 85 metres wide. The weir's falling waters can be heard clearly in Ham on a still night. The weir's purpose is to keep the seawater which comes up the tidal River Thames from mixing with the fresh river water further upstream. Much of London's water supply comes from the river upstream from Teddington and Hampton where the water works are situated. There are three locks and the backwater presents a picturesque and lively scene with its varied craft, including many houseboats.

One page 18:
British Aerospace, which occupies a riverside site at the southern end of Ham Lands

On page 16:
Ham Lands with Eel Pie Island bottom right

On page 19:
Teddington Lock with the Thames Television Studios in the foreground

**Ham and Petersham** both have many historic houses, as the royal connections of the area attracted many aristocratic families, such as Dysarts, lords of the manor of both Ham and Petersham and their Scottish connections due to the Duke of Lauderdale, the second husband of Elizabeth Countess of Dysart.

This couple was responsible for the refurbishment in the 1670s of **Ham House**, built in 1610, so that it became a jewel of late 17th century interior design. But Ham House is only one of the many 17th & 18th century houses which were built near the Petersham Road. Some, such as Bute House and Petersham Lodge, were demolished in the 19th century, but Montrose House, at the right-angled bend of the road near River Lane, and Sudbrook House, a Palladian building now the clubhouse of a golf club, still remain, together with others (such as Ormeley Lodge) also in private hands.

**Ham House**, however, can be visited (except on Mondays) and is immensely rewarding. Since the National Trust took over the house in 1948, it has blossomed, losing the somewhat grim and forbidding look it had formerly.

The Victoria & Albert Museum administered the house up to 1991 and the policy was to restore both house and gardens to their original splendour, as if the Duke and Duchess of Lauderdale were still there. The Duchess may well have been arrogant and ambitious, with a character driven to extremes, so that she was described by a contemporary as "a violent friend and a much more violent enemy", while her husband was unprepossessing, unscrupulous and crafty, but both were learned and clever, and together they created an environment of luxury and elegance. In the time of Charles II, the house was renowned as one of the finest villas in the country.

There is much of interest to see at Ham, including many objects used by the Lauderdales themselves. The V & A have gathered together other examples of furniture, and modern reproductions of the original wall-hangings and curtains have been made where the originals have not survived, but this policy has been followed only to complete the furnishing of certain rooms so as to show off the house to best advantage.

The visitor cannot help but be fascinated by the richness of decoration and by the taste and elegance displayed by the aristocratic owners. Among many features of interest are the paintings displayed throughout the house, especially the portraits by Lely of the Duchess in her youth and in later life (they are in the Round Gallery) and the portraits of the Charles II period in the Long Gallery, while the Miniature Room contains an interesting collection of miniatures from Elizabeth I's time onwards.

The grounds of Ham House have also been undergoing restoration. The aim of the National Trust has been to reproduce features of the late 17th century and early 18th century gardens, stocking them with trees and plants known to have been grown at Ham. Summer-houses similar to those shown in an engraving of 1739 have been built in the four hedged enclosures in the Wilderness which lies beyond the terrace and lawns of the South Front.

VISITS: *OPEN TUES - SUN. 11.00 - 17.00. CLOSED MONDAYS (EXCEPT BANK HOLIDAYS), GOOD FRIDAY, CHRISTMAS DAY, BOXING DAY AND NEW YEAR'S DAY. REFRESHMENTS AVAILABLE (IN THE ROSE GARDEN IN SUMMER). NATIONAL TRUST SHOP.*

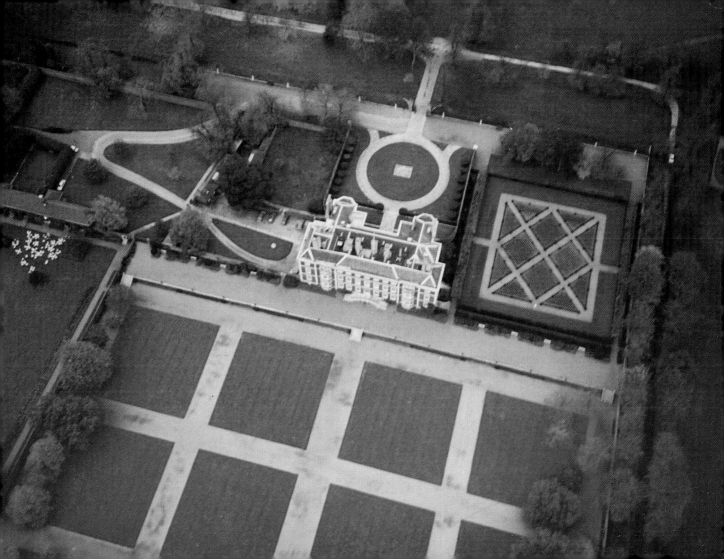

Adjoining Ham House grounds is **Ham Polo field.** Although polo as a game has connotations of privilege and exclusiveness, it must be said that to the ordinary spectator, polo at Ham has a friendly and relaxed atmosphere.

From the landing stage on the river bank near Ham House a **ferry** still piles across the river from the Twickenham side to Ham. Daily 10.00 - 18.00. This is a great boon to residents and visitors wishing to cross to Twickenham (or vice-versa) since it avoids a very long detour by road, and nowadays Hammerton's ferry is in operation throughout the year with the exception of Christmas Day. If you are on the Ham side you have to stand at the top of the steps and wave! Soon the boat will come chugging across. As you cross the river sitting just above the level of the water, it is hard to escape the feeling of being part of a long tradition - a ferry has been in operation here since at least the 17th century.

**Twickenham Riverside**

This is a lively and appealing section of the river's course with much visual interest, and a popular location for local artists. Pubs like the White Swan and the Barmy Arms add local colour and look across to Eel Pie Island with its busy boatyards. Nowadays the sound of hammering and the chinking of chains are about the loudest noises to issue from Eel Pie Island, but earlier in the century it had a raffish atmosphere and summer nights would resound to the throb of dance music as young people flocked to its hotel. Modern houses have now been built on Eel Pie Island, though some of the earlier wooden chalet-type summer houses still remain.

On page 30:
Twickenham Riverside with Church Lane
The Barmy Arms pub faces the embankment

On page 22:
Eel Pie Island

**The Twickenham riverside** has many houses of considerable historic interest, including Strawberry Hill, York House, Orleans House and Marble Hill House. All of these are now used for different purposes from those for which they were first intended.

**Strawberry Hill** was built by Horace Walpole in the middle of the 18th century. He had the idea of building a medieval castle on a small scale, and from this idea grew the "Gothic" house with its turrets and battlements, its fan-vaulting and stained glass. But the interior has a lightness which bears witness to its 18th century origin. Walpole's Gothic house became very fashionable and contributed to the later craze for "Gothic" fantasy at the end of the century.

**Strawberry Hill** is now occupied by a Training College and can be visited only by appointment.

**York House** was once the home of Edward Hyde, Earl of Clarendon, who was Lord Chancellor to Charles II and incidentally grandfather to two Queens of England, Mary and Anne, through his daughter Anne Hyde who married James Duke of York. Clarendon was accustomed to travelling by river from York House to Hampton Court when Charles II was in residence there.

In mid-Victorian times York House became a royal residence for the Comte de Paris. A later owner, and Indian tycoon Sir Ratan Tata, enlivened the gardens with an elaborate fountain with nymphs and winged horses, which can be glimpsed from the river walk. York House is now used for municipal offices.

**Orleans House**, a little further along the riverside, nowadays is represented only by the Octagon Room, used for exhibitions, and a picture gallery now stands where the mansion once stood. In 1800, Louis Philippe, Duke of Orleans came to live here in exile from France and the name of the house was changed in his honour. Twickenham was a centre for Orleanist emigres again later in the 19th century.

*VISITS:*     *TUES - SAT 13.00 - 17.30; SUN 14.00 TO 17.00. CLOSES AT 16.30 OCT - MAR. GARDENS OPEN DAILY 9.00 - SUNSET. ADMISSION FREE*

More remains of **Marble Hill House**, which is a few minutes walk away facing the river.

Marble Hill is an elegant small Palladian villa, built by Henrietta Howard, Countess of Suffolk, long-time mistress of George II. Her neighbour, the poet Alexander Pope, described her as "a reasonable woman, handsome, witty, yet a friend". Indeed she had many friends and she was pleased to entertain them at Marble Hill to which she had escaped from the boredom of court life. Pope designed the gardens at Marble Hill, and built an underground grotto decorated with shells and semi-precious stones (a craze in the 18th century). This was similar to the one he had built for himself in his house nearby. At the present time Lady Suffolk's grotto is to be reconstructed in the garden as part of a general refurbishment of the house and grounds.

Since 1974 a number of paintings of Rome by Panini, once part of the house's heritage, have been found, purchased, and returned to Marble Hill. The damask bedchamber has been restored and a mahogany four-poster bed purchased for it. Crimson flock wallpaper has been specially reproduced from fragments of 18th century paper used by the same decorator at Lydiard Park in Wiltshire. Regilding of the main reception room, repainting, and the installation of new lighting, using fibre optic tubes, have all contributed to Marble Hill being awarded a Diploma of Merit by Europa Nostra, a federation of 200 conservation concerns in 22 European countries. This is a recognition of the restoration work done at Marble Hill since 1966 by English Heritage.

*VISITS:*  *SAT - THURS 10.00 - 17.00*
*SUN 14.00 - 17.00. CLOSES*
*16.00 NOVEMBER - JANUARY*
*ADMISSION FREE.*

## Richmond

Crossing Richmond Bridge (the oldest surviving Thames Bridge in London, built in 1777) is to enter a town conscious of its own distinction and distinctiveness. Though surrounded now by great stretches of West London, Richmond is nevertheless no suburb; it has always retained its identity as an independent Surrey town.

Contributing to this is its **situation** on the river route to Windsor, and its **site**, sheltered by the great river cliff of Richmond Hill. The town is sandwiched between the vast open spaces of Richmond Park and the river bank itself, along which stretches a promenade which has for centuries been a fashionable public walk, and which is at its best on a sunny summer's day when it is possible to sit at one of the waterside pubs and watch the busy life of the river.

The rehabilitation of the decrepit buildings which for so many years were an eyesore between Water Lane and the Bridge, has been accomplished very much to the satisfaction of most of Richmond's inhabitants, though not without controversy, since the scheme (by Quinlan Terry) has involved building in a revived Classical style. The series of facades has been sensitively orchestrated to produce a harmonious and satisfying whole, particularly effective when seen from the river, where the buildings are fronted by lawns crossed by zigzag paths. Here is the landing stage where the Queen stepped from her barge with its red-coated Tudor bargemen, when she came to open the Riverside Development on Oct. 28th 1988.

The Old Town hall in Whittaker Avenue is now the home of the Richmond Museum and reference rooms, while on the ground floor near the Tourist Information centre is the Riverside Coffee Shop with its attractive view of the river, and, usually, also an interesting exhibition of some artistic nature.

The main shopping street of Richmond is George Street and its extension the Quadrant, but Richmond's special feature is the series of alleys connecting George Street with the Green, where are to be found the specialist shops which make a visit to Richmond so interesting.

Henry VIII's old Palace was situated between the river and the Green, which was originally a royal jousting ground. Nothing of the old palace remains except the Gatehouse and, through this gateway into the Old Palace Yard, the three surviving buildings of the Old Wardrobe Elizabeth I died at Richmond in 1603, reputedly

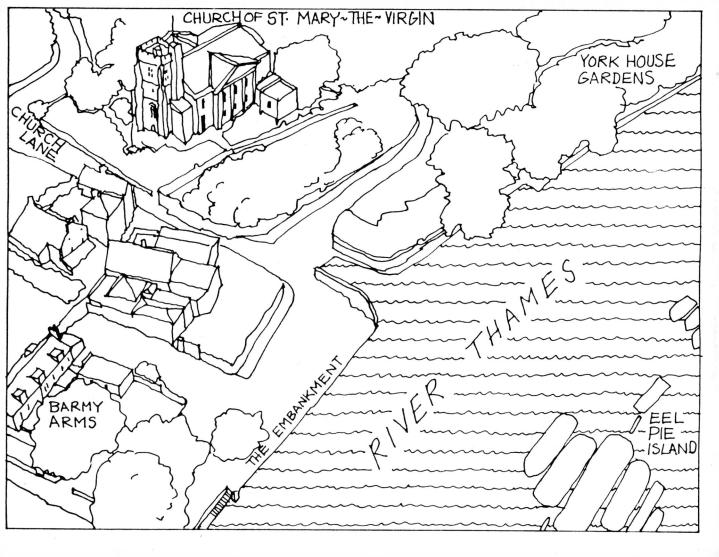

CHURCH OF ST. MARY~THE~VIRGIN

YORK HOUSE GARDENS

CHURCH LANE

RIVER THAMES

THE EMBANKMENT

BARMY ARMS

EEL ~PIE~ ISLAND

in one of the upstairs rooms of the Gatehouse.

Nevertheless many historic houses remain, near to the Green and around it. Trumpeter's House, built in 1701, (now divided into private apartments), has an imposing portico facing the river which can be seen from the riverside walk.

Notable on the Green itself is Maids of Honour Row, built in 1723 to house the maids of honour of Caroline, wife of the future George II. Now private houses, their interiors retain decorations and relics from their illustrious past.

Buildings of different periods surround the Green, most of them fitting in with the historic setting. The exception is a recent addition on the northern side where the school of thought which supports the idea that architecture should always be contemporary won the day with a row of houses built in 1970. It is difficult not to feel that these houses do not live up to their prestigious setting.

Another interesting series of shops climbs up Richmond Hill, eventually giving way to houses of a quality commensurate with their position on a hill which commands one of the best views in the whole of England, one painted by Reynolds and Turner and by a thousand other artists. The hill ends with the Richmond Hill Hotel, and theRichmond Gate Hotel, and overlooks the luxurious Petersham Hotel with its striking architecture.

Opposite to the entrance to Richmond Park stands the dominating Star and Garter Home for disabled war veterans. This site has been occupied in former times by several successive hostelries of the same name. One was burned down in 1870 and was replaced by a hotel with a ballroom and restaurants. This in turn was demolished in 1920 and the Star & Garter Home built in a neo-classical style.

On page 33:
The new development, Richmond

On page 34:
The Petersham Hotel with the Star and Garter Home for Disabled Servicemen behind it

**Richmond Park** with its woodland, its enclosed plantations such as the Isabella plantation (at its best in May and June) and its herds of red deer and fallow deer, presents a setting of almost endless fascination. With its 2000 acres and immense variety, it would take a lifetime to exhaust its possibilities of interest. Lucky indeed are the students of the Royal Ballet School, now housed in White Lodge, a royal residence once the home in her youth of Queen Mary, mother of Edward VIII and George VI.

Pembroke Lodge is equally interesting, and was once the home of Bertrand Russell, whose father Lord John Russell was granted the tenancy by Queen Victoria when he was Prime Minister. This is now a busy and popular café, where refreshments can be eaten in the imposing rooms, or taken out of doors, overlooking the terraced gardens and with the splendid view over Petersham and Ham spread out at one's feet.

Downstream from Richmond another meander of the Thames encloses **the Old Deer Park** and **Kew Gardens** on the right bank of the river, while opposite lies the equally green and open land of **Syon Park**.

Alongside the Old Deer Park is a golf course, with a practice driving ground and nearby is a leisure centre with baths and water chutes. This is the site mooted for a new Richmond Baths complex, (see picture on page 35.)

On page 35:
Richmond Baths in the Old Deer Park

On page 37:
Richmond Green (top)
Along river bank is Cholmondley walk with Asgill House at the left-hand end and Trumpeter's House in centre of picture

**Kew Gardens** occupies the remaining area on the right bank up to Kew Bridge, and contains enough of interest to occupy the casual visitor for a whole day. Those with more specialised or educational tastes could spend much more time than that. There is a useful division of interest between the botanic gardens themselves, with their rare plants and glasshouses, and the historical interest of Kew Palace and Queen Charlotte's cottage.

The size of the gardens themselves is impressive, as is the variety of landscapes, from woodlands and green lawns to the lakes which provide habitats for many water birds. In fine weather there are endless pleasant walks, and something of interest at almost every season of the year. In wet weather, there are the many glasshouses, including the new Princess of Wales conservatory opened in July 1987, which houses 15000 plants in 10 computer-controlled temperature zones.

The Temperate House (seen in the picture) is the largest existing Victorian Conservatory, completed in 1899. Another Victorian conservatory, the Palm House, has recently undergone a total restoration which has taken five years and £8 million. Modern technology has been employed to create tropical forest environments relating to three major world areas - Africa, Asia with Australasia, and the Americas - and will help people to understand the economic repercussions of the destruction of the rainforest. Two new basements have been built, one of which will contain an aquarium for the study of marine plants and algae.

The Orangery, built in 1761, now houses a tea room and the Kew Shop, with a wide selection of books, pictures and gifts. Two other restaurants, the Kew Bakery and the Pavilion Restaurant cater for visitors spending a few hours in the gardens.

On page 38:
The Temperate House at Kew: an autumn scene

The Royal connection of the area surfaces again in Kew Palace, built in 1631, which became the favourite home in the 18th century of George III and Queen Charlotte, where they lived with their numerous children in the style of country gentle folk. George III was interested in the development of Kew Gardens as a home for rare plants, thus continuing the work of Princess Augusta, his mother, widow of Frederick Prince of Wales who died before his father George II. Famous gardeners included William Aiton and Capability Brown (who planted the Rhododendron Dell.)

In 1772 George III built the Queen's Cottage for Charlotte. This is at the opposite end of the Gardens and was originally conceived as a summer-house. It can also be visited during the summer months. In spring it is surrounded by bluebells.

Since the death of Queen Charlotte in 1818, the Kew Palaces have not been inhabited, though Queen Victoria made many additions to the gardens, which were given to the nation in 1841 and subsequently entered on their great period of international reputation.

There is so much to see at Kew that the map provided on entering the gardens is invaluable.

*VISITS:* *OPEN THROUGHOUT THE YEAR 10.00 - 16.00, WITH LATER OPENINGS UP TO 20.00 IN JULY AND AUGUST.*

On page 39:
The new Princess of Wales Conservatory

On page 42:
The Palm House

Across the river from Kew can be seen **Syon House**. This can be approached from Twickenham Bridge via the riverside near Isleworth Ait. Opposite the Ait is the **London Apprentice**, a 500 year-old pub which took its name from the apprentices of the City Livery companies who used to row upstream to this inn which was a mecca for lightermen and boatmen.

**Syon House** is sign-posted nearby. The original foundation was a convent suppressed by Henry VIII at the Dissolution of the Monasteries. Catherine Howard was imprisoned here before her execution, and Syon subsequently passed through several hands including the Duke of Northumberland, father-in-law to Lady Jane Grey, who sailed in state down river from Syon to her tragic destiny as the Nine Day Queen.

Syon eventually came into the hands of the Percy family. Henry Percy became Earl of Northumberland, but this earl was no relation to the earlier Duke who had proclaimed Lady Jane Grey queen. George III created a later earl Duke of Northumberland and Syon House still belongs to, and is lived in by, his descendants.

The outside is still Tudor in appearance but this is no preparation for the classical magnificence of the interior, which was remodelled by Robert Adam. It remains his most brilliant work. The Great Hall with its floor of black and white marble, its pale walls adorned with classical figures, leads to the Ante-Room, in Roman style with huge columns of green marble which were dredged up from the River Tiber in Rome. The splendour and perfection of this room is not surpassed by any of the great houses of the country, such as Blenheim Palace or Holkham Hall.

Syon also has a considerable number of Stuart portraits of great interest, and a Long Gallery altered very skilfully by Adam from the old Elizabethan gallery.

On page 43:
Syon House

Syon has many other features of interest for example its gardens dominated by a huge glass conservatory built in 1821 (see picture page 46); its garden centre opened in 1968; and its Butterfly House opened in 1981.

*VISITS:*     *SYON HOUSE ITSELF IS OPEN FROM GOOD FRIDAY OR APRIL 1ST (WHICHEVER IS EARLIER) TO SEPTEMBER 28TH SUN - THURS 12.00 - 17.00.*
*OCTOBER: SUNDAYS ONLY GARDENS: OPEN ALL THE YEAR (EXCEPT CHRISTMAS DAY AND*

*BOXING DAY) MAR - OCT 10.00 - 18.00. OCT - FEB 10.00 - DUSK.*

Before reaching Kew Bridge the Thames is joined by the Grand Union Canal. Here the north bank has been developed with the building of the Waterman's Arts Centre.

At Kew Bridge the River Thames begins to turn eastwards, around Chiswick and Barnes, traversing the bends so familiar to spectators of the Boat Race. Here our story ends.

On page 43:
Syon House

On page 46:
The magnificent conservatory at Syon, with the modern garden centre

**Acknowledgements:** We would like to thank the model aircraft and helicopter pilot Martin Allen S.M.A.E. (A & B Certs) for his patience and expertise in flying the model aircraft from which these photographs were taken by remote controlled camera.

Inner back (page 48)  -  The River Thames showing Ham House (right bank), Orleans House (left bank, centre), Marble Hill House (top left)